Prayer Paws

Developed from an original idea by Pete James

Based on original designs and initial television artwork
by Noah Warnes and Missional Generation.

Published by **Candle Books**
www.lionhudson.com
Part of the SPCK Group
SPCK, 36 Causton Street, London, SW1P 4ST

ISBN 978 1 78128 460 5

First edition 2023

Acknowledgments
Designed by aitch:creative Ltd. www.aitchcreative.co.uk

Artwork from animations by Three Arrows Media

A catalogue record for this book is available from the British Library

Produced on paper from sustainable sources.

Printed and bound in China, April 2023,
by Dream Colour (Hong Kong) Printing Limited

Cheeky pandas®

Prayer Paws

Written and adapted by
Paul Kerensa
& **Pete James**

CANDLE
BOOKS

About the Cheeky Pandas®

Cheeky Pandas® provide free online resources to help children and families grow in their faith. The songs, music videos, cartoons, and devotionals are fun, bright, professionally written and produced. Families, churches, and ministries around the world can access and directly watch these resources.

To hear the songs from the song machine and to watch the full animated episodes go to:

www.cheekypandas.com

Why not pick up a **Cheeky Pandas®** storybook?

The Bouncy Castle	The Best Present Ever	The Day Off	The Drum Machine	The Lost Voice
ISBN 978 1 78128 455 1	ISBN 978 1 78128 452 0	ISBN 978 1 78128 453 7	ISBN 978 1 78128 456 8	ISBN 978 1 78128 459 9

Contents

Let's get ready to **Praise God...**

6

with words from our **hearts**.

Point Up!

Praise God for being so wonderful,

so big, and so powerful.

All things are possible for God.

9

Look UP!

Praise God, who made the world,

all the stars, and everything in space.

Look around!

Praise God, who made the plants,

all the animals, and every one of us.

Dear God,

Thank you that we can have joy
knowing we're loved by you.
Thank you that we can enjoy
playing and praising you together.

Thank you, God, for this new day.

14

Rain or shine, we'll follow your way.

welcome

Each new day

is like opening a box from

the Pandaroo delivery.

Full of surprises and

things to do!

Awesome!

Chat to God about what you will be doing today.

Ask God to help you to do your best through the day.

FRAGILE

Pandaroo

Thank you, God,

that we can chat to you

at any time, anywhere,

and about everything.

"I like chatting to God because..."

Ask God to help you to listen too.

Thank you, Jesus,

for being our special friend.

Thank you for always looking out for us,

which makes us happy in our hearts.

Help us be a good friend to others.

Dear God,

Thank you for everything we enjoy
but thank you for Jesus most of all.
Help us to spread this joy to others.

Dear God,

Thank you for the people we love.

Thank you for loving us first,

loving us just the way we are,

and showing us how

to love others.

Make a paper chain of
Cheeky Pandas and write
the names of your family
and friends on each one.

Trace

Fold

Chat to God about your family and friends.
Ask God to bless them and love them too.

23

Thank you, God,

for the food we eat, the clothes we wear, and the homes we live in. Help those who are hungry, and cold, and without a home.

Thank you, God,

for our thoughts and ideas.
Help us to make the world a
better place to live in and
to share with others.

Thank you, God,

for our gifts and talents.
Help us to use them to
show others how much
you love them too.

Chat to God about what
you like doing.

Ask God to do more with your talents.

Sometimes we **feel down**

and can't explain how we are feeling.

Thank you, God,

that we can chat to you and other people who care about us too.

Chat to God about how you are feeling.

Draw your own panda face,

If you are feeling sad, ask God to help you feel

better, safe, and to take all your fears away.

Thank you, God,

for listening when we feel
confused or hurt.
We trust you to help
make things better.

Thank you

for other people we trust,
who listen to us too.
Help us to forgive others
when they hurt us.

Please help us, God...

to learn from you in all we think, and say, and do.

Sometimes our lives can be a **muddle.**

We may feel angry with ourselves and others.

Help us to stay calm because you can help

us through.

OOPS!

Chat to God
about your troubles.

Ask God to help your
troubles drift away.

Sorry, God,

for the things that we have said and
done that have hurt others and you.

Chat to God about

what you are sorry for.

POP!

Thank you
for forgiving me.

Dear God,

Help us to be faithful
to you and to each other,
just like you are perfectly
faithful to us.
Help us to keep
our promises,
look after other people, and
make sure no one is left out.

When life feels tough and we don't know what to do next ...

help us to keep going and guide us along the right path.

Follow the trail with your finger through the maze.

At each turn, chat to God about things that are hard.

Ask God to help you to keep trying.

Dear God,

Help us to be kind and loving to one another.

Thank you for being so kind and loving to us.

Let us help one another, and give to one another,

and share with one another all that you have given us.

FRAGILE

PANDAROO

Dear God,

When we get frustrated with things,

please give us patience.

Thank you for being patient and kind to us.

Help us to take time and trust you in all we do.

We **think** of others in this world.

The whole world is in **God's hands.**

The world is a big place, but

God looks after everyone.

God bless those who are lonely or unwell.

Make some paper planes, write the names
of the people you are thinking about
on them, and let the planes fly.

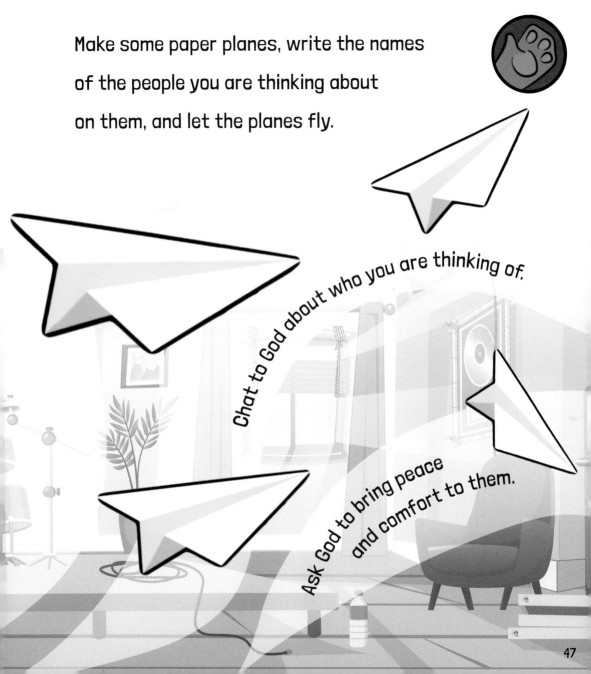

Chat to God about who you are thinking of.

Ask God to bring peace
and comfort to them.

The world around us can be a noisy place.

Take a moment to find some peace and quiet.

Close your eyes.

Breathe in deeply.

Know that God is with you.

Breathe out.

God brings you peace.

Amen.